STEAM JOB? DREAM JOB!

JOBS IN TECHNOLOGY

By Bethany Latham

KidHaven PUBLISHING

Published in 2026 by
KidHaven Publishing, an Imprint of
Greenhaven Publishing, LLC
2544 Clinton St., Buffalo, NY 14224

Written by: Bethany Latham
Edited by: Rebecca Phillips-Bartlett
Designed by: Rob Delph

All facts, statistics, web addresses, and URLs in this book were verified as valid and accurate at time of writing. No responsibility for any changes to external websites or references can be accepted by either the author or publisher.

Cataloging-in-Publication Data

Names: Latham, Bethany.
Title: Jobs in technology / Bethany Latham.
Description: Buffalo, NY : KidHaven Publishing, 2026. | Series: STEAM job? Dream job! | Includes glossary and index.
Identifiers: ISBN 9781534552241 (pbk.) | ISBN 9781534552258 (library bound) | ISBN 9781534552265 (ebook)
Subjects: LCSH: Technology--Vocational guidance--Juvenile literature.
Classification: LCC T65.3 L384 2026 | DDC 602.3--dc23

Printed in China

CPSIA compliance information: Batch #QW26KH: For further information contact Greenhaven Publishing LLC at 1-844-317-7404.

Please visit our website, www.greenhavenpublishing.com.
For a free color catalog of all our high-quality books, call toll free 1-844-317-7404 or fax 1-844-317-7405.

Find us on

IMAGE CREDITS

Images courtesy of Shutterstock.com, unless otherwise stated.

Cover – Pavlo S, YamabikaY, SeventyFour, Nsit, ST.art, fiestachka. 2–3 – Gorodenkoff, EKKAPHAN CHIMPALEE, Kobee. 4–5 – Budimir Jevtic, PeopleImages.com – Yuri A, kelvn, Wayhome Studio, wavebreakmedia, ST.art. 6–7 – LALAKA, Andrey_Popov, EKKAPHAN CHIMPALEE. 8–9 – wee dezign, Joyseulay, ST.art. 10–11 – Gorodenkoff, ArtHub02. 12–13 – Teerapong mahawan, Maximumm, Kobee. 14–15 – Dmitry Kalinovsky, Frame Stock Footage, Nsit. 16–17 – Hardyguardy, Summit Art Creations, THICHA SATAPITANON. 18–19 – DC Studio, vs148. 20–21 – Oleksandr Nagaiets, Sura Nualpradid, fiestachka. 22–23 – Roman Samborskyi, PeopleImages.com – Yuri A, Sumala Chidchoi, Nsit, riabchevskii. 24 – Nsit, fiestachka. Vectors used throughout – Pavlo S, YamabikaY.

CONTENTS

Words that look like **this** can be found in the glossary on page 24.

ALL ABOUT STEAM

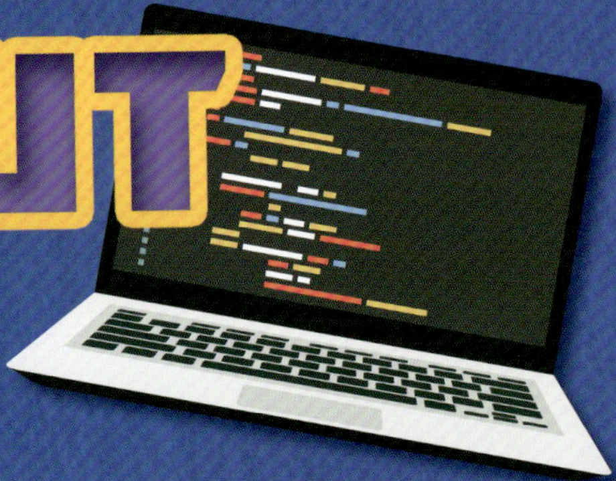

There are many amazing jobs in the world. Do you know what job you want to have when you grow up? STEAM **careers** use science, technology, engineering, the arts, and math.

STEAM careers cover many different fields. They include jobs in medicine, music, gaming, and more. The skills you learn in STEAM classes at school can help you get a great job when you grow up.

ALL ABOUT TECHNOLOGY

Technology involves using scientific knowledge to help people do tasks. Technology careers usually involve working with electronic machines such as computers. People who work with technology might design things such as websites.

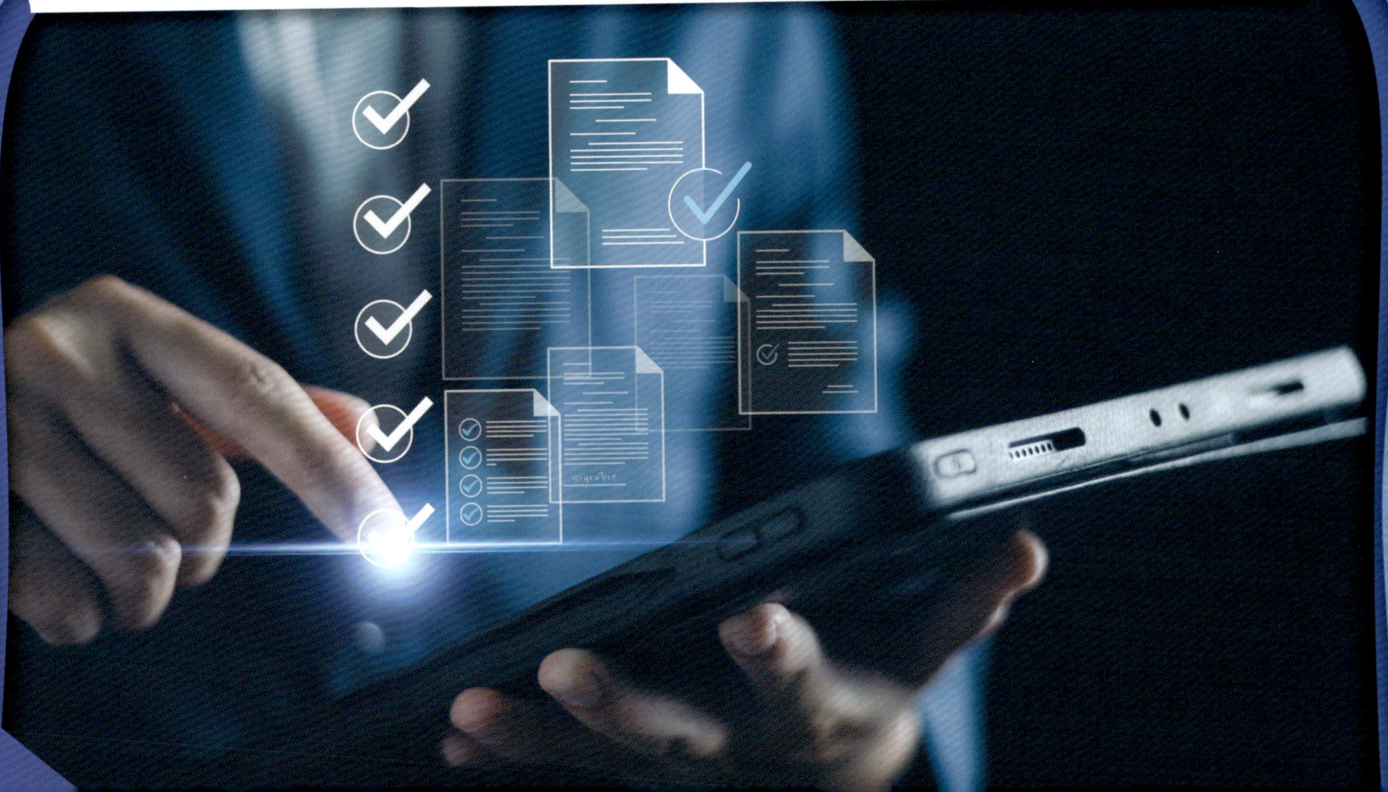

BE INSPIRED!

LET'S TAKE A LOOK AT SOME DREAM JOBS IN TECHNOLOGY!

Technology careers often include working with **digital** information, or data. Data can be used in many different ways.

Technology can also be used for fun and entertainment. Video games are an example.

SOFTWARE DEVELOPER

Software is a set of **programs** that tells a computer what to do. Software developers create software to do specific jobs. For example, websites are made using software.

Software developers write and test the computer **code** that makes software work. They fix any problems that stop it from working. Software developers must be good at problem solving. They also need good math skills.

DATABASE ADMINISTRATOR

Database administrators make and manage computer **systems** that store data. These are called databases. Database administrators are in charge of keeping the data safe. They make sure only certain people can see the information.

Database administrators make sure databases are easy to use. They think of ways to make them safer. Database administrators must be good at math and know how to write computer code.

ELECTRONICS TECHNICIAN

Electronics technicians make sure that electronic **equipment** works properly. They often set up electronic systems and machines and fix them when they break. Electronics technicians usually work with electronic hardware.

HARDWARE IS THE PHYSICAL PARTS OF AN ELECTRONIC MACHINE.

Sometimes, electronics technicians design and build electronic equipment. They can work in many different areas, including telecommunications. Telecommunications includes telephones and the internet. Electronics technicians need skills in math, computer technology, and engineering.

GAME TESTER

Game testers play video games before they are sold, Game testers make sure video games work well and are fun to play. They look for bugs in the games.

A BUG IS A MISTAKE IN A COMPUTER PROGRAM'S CODE.

BE INSPIRED!

THINK ABOUT THE GAMES YOU PLAY. WHAT MAKES THEM ENJOYABLE?

Game testers tell the people designing the game about any problems they find. They often play the game more than once to make sure it works properly. Game testers need patience and good computer skills.

APP DEVELOPER

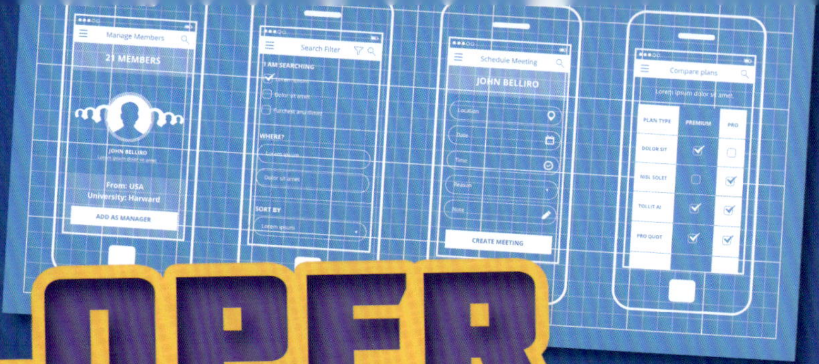

APP IS SHORT FOR APPLICATION.

App developers make applications for smartphones, tablets, and computers. Apps include games, calendars, video players, and more. App developers write the code that allows the app to work.

App developers fix any bugs they find and **update** the apps to make them better. App developers usually focus on one area, such as smartphone apps. They must be creative and good at math.

BE INSPIRED!

ASK QUESTIONS ABOUT HOW DIFFERENT APPS WORK.

CYBERSECURITY SPECIALIST

Cybersecurity specialists keep digital systems and information safe. They try to prevent cybercrime. Cybercrime is crime that happens digitally. Cybersecurity specialists look at the ways people commit cybercrime and try to stop it.

Schools, banks, and **governments** all need cybersecurity specialists. These specialists need to have knowledge of computers and good problem-solving skills.

LIGHTING TECHNICIAN

Lighting technicians usually work at live events, such as concerts and theater performances. They set up the lights. During performances, lighting technicians sit in the **lighting booth** and control the lights.

BE INSPIRED!

ASK QUESTIONS ABOUT HOW LIGHTING IS USED IN LIVE SHOWS.

Some lighting technicians work in film and television. They use lights to make things look good on camera. Lighting technicians need lots of experience to know how different lights work.

THE POWER OF STEAM

We have looked at some amazing technology careers, but there are many more. Technology is always changing. New things are being created all the time. Technology is an exciting career to get into!

BE INSPIRED!

HOW CAN YOU USE STEAM TO CHANGE THE WORLD?

There are many things you can do with technology when you grow up. It is important to work hard in all the STEAM subjects. This is because STEAM subjects often connect to each other.

GLOSSARY

CAREERS	job areas that can be worked in for a large amount of a person's life
CODE	instructions for a computer to follow written in a language a computer can understand
DIGITAL	written and stored on an machine such as a computer
EQUIPMENT	items that are needed to complete a certain job
GOVERNMENTS	groups of people with the power to run countries and decide their laws
LIGHTING BOOTH	the place where the lighting technician sits during a performance to control the stage lights
PHYSICAL	able to be seen and touched
PROGRAMS	lists of instructions that tell a computer to do something
SYSTEMS	sets of things that work together to do specific jobs
UPDATE	to change something in a way that makes it more up to date

INDEX